Our world of sustainability
through the eyes of Gizmo the cat

From where I see it

Lubb, Gizmo

Assisted by
Karen Olson Johnson

Contents
(This is what's in my book!)

My Observations 8—167
(well that's it really but . . .)

Gizmosims 168
(my personal glossary of words)

Gratitude 169
(thanking people— mind you it was me who did all this you know)

Outroduction 170
(something the Lady insisted on writing)

Conclusion 171
(short and sweet like me)

Appendix 172
(usful stuff for teachers)

Bio 175
(All about the Lady, but nothing about me!)

Feedback 175
(What's this? Something to do with sound?)

Dedication

This book is dedicated to my mates:
Basil and Radar 🐾 Holly 🐾 Roland
Hermoinie 🐾 Elvis 🐾 Princess 🐾 Kierara
Puffer 🐾 Boris 🐾 Harry 🐾 Fred 🐾 Romeo
Lily 🐾 Mama 🐾 Glinda 🐾 Pumpkin
Kally 🐾 Meeko 🐾 Hershey 🐾 Vato
Precious 🐾 Gatsby 🐾 Isabelle
Precious Angel 🐾 Buddy 🐾 Screech
Bright Eyes 🐾 Tigger 🐾 Oreo 🐾 Tino
Molly 🐾 Cinnamon 🐾 Twinkle 🐾 Rudy
Phantom 🐾 Rascal 🐾 Muffin 🐾 Scooter
Archie 🐾 Luna 🐾 Sherry 🐾 Tom
Julius the Lion King 🐾 Squeeks 🐾 Jerry
Aphrodite 🐾 Daisy 🐾 Trucker 🐾 Ivy
Little Red Kitty 🐾 Cat 🐾 Magic 🐾 Aura
Danger Mouse 🐾 Jasper 🐾 Jules 🐾 Figaro
Cornelia 🐾 Dusty 🐾 Alice 🐾 Diamond
Orville 🐾 Hershel 🐾 Sunny 🐾 Emily
Sooty and Azure Blue 🐾 AND all the
other kitties (and those who love them)
of this world,

Luff, Gizmo 🐾 🐾

You will notice all those funny boxy black and white squares.

They are QR codes!!!

Point your smart phone at them and wambo you are at a website. Cool huh?

Try it!!

Let me introduce myself

As you may have figured out I'm Gizmo. I love to observe the world through my very own personal cable network channel. The screen is huge. It is about the size of a glass patio door, and through it I watch the world go by. Mostly, I watch the birds, the squirrels, and the giant rabbits.

I have learned to become very observant by sitting and being very still. My observational skills have become so good that I am now using them on my humans in our home. They do some interesting things around here. I'm going to tell you about some of 'em 'cuz I think you just might want to know. My tremendous powers of observation will serve you well.

Keeping you posted,

Luff, Gizmo

7

Dear Little Ones

In my home, I carefully watch my humans as they go about their day-to-day routines. My humans are the Lady and the Big One. They live with me in my wonderful home.

One thing I have noticed lately is that my humans no longer buy yogurt (yummm) in those little containers. They now buy the yogurt in a big container. Then they take some out of that big container, put it in a small jar, and mix in their own fruit. My favorite fruit is mango. Have you tried it?

I've seen them put this mixture in their lunch bags. I know the trash isn't filling up nearly as fast, so I think this is a smart human move. I will watch for more of these moves and keep you in the loop.

8   Luff, Gizmo

Little Yogurt

Little Yogurt

Little Yogurt

Little Yogurt

Little Yogurt

Little Yogurt

Little Yogurt

Little Yogurt

BIG YOGURT

9

What about us humans?

Take a look around your home. Do you have lots of small containers in your kitchen, laundry, and bathroom? Do these products come in larger, more economical, and ultimately more Earth friendly versions? Consider making small changes week by week as you go about purchasing products. Perhaps start with something like yogurt and then think about other products like shampoo or toothpaste. Buying these in the largest containers possible (maybe in bulk purchasing) and ensuring the containers are safe and recyclable is a win-win. This is a common sense for common good move that is great for the pocketbook and for the planet.

Alright, let's really do something . . .

Adults – Get serious about containers. Drastically reduce the trash you generate by reducing the number of containers you purchase. If the product you select is in a container that cannot be recycled, do not buy it. Pay close attention to what you would do with a product *and* its container once you bring it home and take it out of the bag. Do you have to dispose of a bunch of containers once the product is consumed?

Kids – Keep track of all the containers you throw away for one week. Make a list and watch how much trash you actually throw away. Ask yourself what changes you can make to reduce your trash.

Together – Discover where "away" is. Research the Great Pacific Garbage Patch.

For more info . . .

The Great Pacific Garbage Patch:
http://goo.gl/nIFB7

Reduce home trash:
http://goo.gl/cEj1Z

Hey, Small Fry,

I am spotting some blinking lights, especially in the kitchen. My humans have an interesting way of making the lights blink.

Before they put something in that big black box and push all the buttons that squeak, they put the long tail into the wall. They say they are plugging it in and out of the wall because of vampires. They plug the tail into the wall and the

lights on the box blink.
They put some food into
the box. Then they push
the squeaking buttons
and wait for a bit. After
they take the food out of the box, the
lights blink until they pull the tail
out of the wall.

OBSERVATION 2

I like the blinking lights. I have seen
them on some other boxes in the living
room. This must be a smart human
move because I certainly haven't seen
any vampires.

Luff, Gizmo

What about us humans?

Phantom energy (or vampire energy, as it is sometimes called) can be a major drain on our household energy use. This is energy that we are wasting without realizing what we are doing. Think of all the appliances and gadgets that have electronic lights and all the equipment that requires charging, and you have identified only some of the phantom energy culprits in your home.

Take just a few seconds to unplug those items, or turn them off at the wall socket, and the energy savings will start to add up. This is a common sense move that could save huge amounts of energy if we all adopted this simple habit. Energy needs to be conserved and used wisely if we are to move toward sustainable lives together, lives of common good.

Alright, let's really do something . . .

Adults – Do an experiment. Figure out how long it takes to really charge your cell phone and then unplug it after it has charged.

Kids – Make sure you learn which things can be unplugged after use and then plugged in when you need them. Do not do this without an adult to supervise. Maybe you can teach them a thing or two.

Together – Make some lights blink.

For more info . . .

Avoiding Phantom Power:
http://goo.gl/VFhYy

Check out Energy Savers:
http://goo.gl/e42I0

Check out Phantom Power:
http://goo.gl/WYDkG

Greetings, Possums,

The cool round bowl in the bathroom has many uses. I occasionally nap in it, but I know my humans use it, too.

They put on a brush teeth in the at night. to spit out I am not they turn they like to the bowl down they are water.

some goop and brush their morning and They use the bowl the leftover goop. quite sure why off the water while do this because I watch it run into and disappear the hole. I think trying to save the

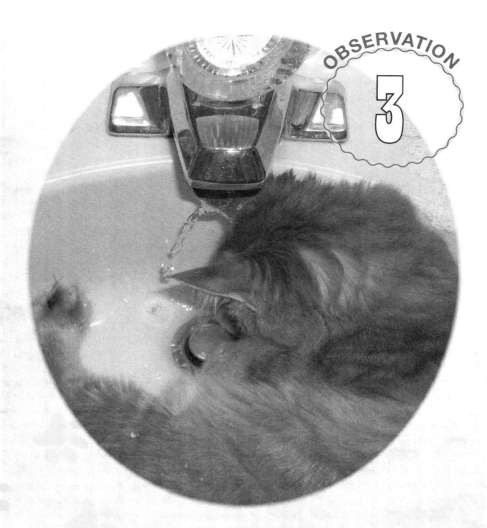

I think this is a smart human move, too, 'cuz water is so cool to watch, I don't want them to run out of it.

Could you tell me what the goop is for, though?

Luff, Gizmo

What about us humans?

Turning off the water while brushing your teeth, or for any kind of cleaning makes good common sense. Lots of water can be wasted by just running down the sink drain while we are doing something else. Just try it once to see how much water is really wasted. The next time you are brushing your teeth, leave the water

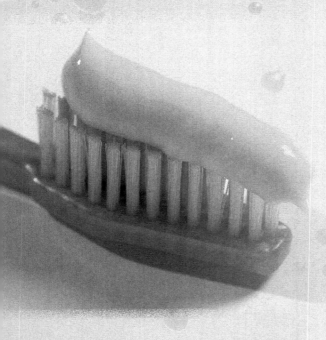

running with the plug in the sink, but watch the water so it does not overflow. You will be amazed how much of this precious resource is lost by not paying attention to simply turning off the water while we are doing a task like brushing our teeth. So many people in the world have no access to clean water. Common sense for common good practice means not being wasteful of the water we have and turning off the faucet.

Alright, let's really do something . . .

Adults – Install an aerator in the faucet of your sink(s). Put in a low-flow shower head or toilet. Wash only full loads of laundry or dishes. Sweep the driveway or walkway. Xeriscape (look it up!) your yard. In other words, quit wasting water and model this behavior.

Kids – When you take a shower, limit your time to 3 minutes. If 3 minutes isn't long enough, then get yourself wet, turn the water off, soap up, and then turn the water on to rinse off.

Together – Discover how people in other parts of the world live without access to running water. How do they adapt?

For more info . . .

Water Conservation:
http://goo.gl/VsCuu

Remember, scan the QR code with your smart phone and it will connect to the website. Cool!

Drop in The Bucket:
http://goo.gl/4CknF

World Water Day:
http://goo.gl/YD8Ud

To the Future,

Every so often this very Cool Lady comes to my front door. She wears this black blanket wrapped around her and she is so nice to me. She gets right down on the floor to pet me and she smells good. She takes one of my humans

with her in her car. I like her because she brings my human back. They say they are going to meetings together in her car and that they are pooling.

I haven't seen either her or my human come back wet, so I do not know what this pooling is for, but they seem to enjoy it. All I care about is that she brings my human back to me.

Luff, Gizmo

What about us humans?

Car pooling is one of the most underutilized forms of energy savings. All you have to do is get on any major roadway in any major metropolitan area in any part of the world to see how underutilized this practice is.

Try starting small by car pooling once or twice a month with someone from work. If you do not travel back and forth to work, (lucky you) try car pooling for shopping or services. It takes a bit of effort in the beginning, but the rewards are huge in terms of fuel savings, let alone wear and tear on vehicles. If we could take a few cars off the road, imagine what could be done for all the traffic nightmares, too. This is a common sense for common good and peace of mind move. And if you are already using mass transit, kudos to you.

Alright, let's really do something . . .

Adults – Find someone with whom to car pool. Try leaving the car at home one day a week, then two, maybe three. Rideshare or ride the bus, light rail, train or subway. See if you can work from home one day a week. Make an effort.

Kids – When going to an activity, find a friend who needs a ride.

Together – Really *try* not to make any unnecessary trips in the family vehicle. When available and appropriate, use mass transit, a bicycle, or your feet. Walk to the store with someone, have a conversation on the way there and back.

For more info . . .

Why Carpool:
http://goo.gl/GbSDM

Carpooling Basics:
http://goo.gl/QLGtf

23

My Imps,

I am anxiously awaiting wash day. Will they or won't they use the foldy thing for the socks? They seem to be using it more and more as the weather changes. Maybe they can give up the

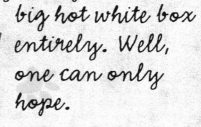

big hot white box entirely. Well, one can only hope.

On days when they decide to not use the big hot white box, they set up the foldy thing downstairs. My humans leave their knickers and socks on the foldy thing for about a day or so. This is plenty of time for me to have my pick of the hanging items. I wait until the coast is clear and then I get to work. Do they call this game hide and seek?

I love it when they do not use the big
hot white box to dry their clothes.
Smart human move and great cat play
time all rolled into one. I gotta think
of more places to hide the socks.

Luff, Gizmo   25

What about us humans?

Trying to be more aware of what clothes you wash and dry can really cut back on energy use. Ask yourself, "Does this really need to be washed and dried or could I just air it out to wear one more time?" This is a common sense move that can save a great deal of money *and* a great deal of energy.

A very effective energy saver is to just let nature do the work of drying your laundry. With the warmth of the sun outside, or simple evaporation inside (as Gizmo prefers), one can save tremendous amounts of electricity or natural gas. This is an easy common sense move that helps the planet and the pocketbook. Besides, there is nothing better than a fresh set of sheets dried outside for a great night's sleep.

Alright, let's really do something . . .

Adults – If you are using the dryer, pay attention. The simple act of taking clothes out before the dryer has stopped and hanging them up can save the use of an iron. Think first before you just toss another load into the dryer. Can this laundry air dry?

Kids – Help your adults with the laundry. Pay special attention to the lint filter and empty it every time you use the dryer. Emptying the filter helps the dryer work more efficiently.

Together – Imagine this: If you had to wash all of your clothes on a rock at the edge of a river and hang them over a bush to dry, might you consider wearing them more than once?

For more info . . .

Project Laundry List:
http://goo.gl/33dct

What's up, Buttercup?

Many an evening rolls from light into dark as I gaze out at the world. Sometimes, I get so carried away in my observations, I lose all track of my humans.

When it is dark outside, though, I know exactly where to find them in our home. They are in the rooms with light. You see, when they move from room to room is the only time I see lights go on and off in our home. They are very easy to track in the night. And when all the lights go out, I still know where my humans are for my eyesight in the dark is very good. Besides, the Big One purrs very loud when he is asleep so I can track him easily.

I think making the lights go on and off for them to see must be another of those smart human moves. I will keep notes on this behavior.

Luff, Gizmo

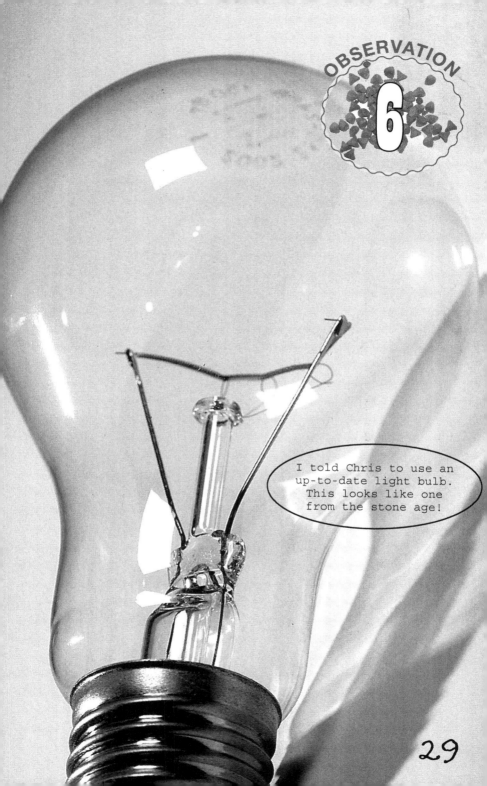

29

What about us humans?

Try making a habit of turning lights on and off as you enter and exit a room or area. This very simple common sense habit can save huge amounts of energy and can be reflected in lower energy bills. If it is difficult to get into the habit, a gentle reminder placed by a light switch for a month or two might help. Sometimes, all we need is a little nudge to be more aware of something simple like this. Changing a bad habit of leaving the lights on into a good habit of turning them off when we are not in the room is a common sense move. If done by enough of us, this could really make a huge collective difference in overall energy consumption. Also, if you work in an office, make sure the lights are off when you leave. Many office buildings sit ablaze with lights left on all night.

Alright, let's really do something . . .

Adults – Many myths exist about whether or not you really save by turning off lights. These are perpetuated by people who don't want to turn off lights. If it really is an issue, try installing sensors.

Kids – Keep track of, and make a list of, all the rooms you move in and out of in any given day that have lights in them. Now, make an effort to turn these lights off when the room is not occupied.

Together – What was life like before we had lights to turn on? Spend some time together in candlelight (with adult supervision). Ask yourself what might be difficult to accomplish without artificial lights to help us in our day-to-day lives? Participate in Earth Hour.

For more info . . .

When to Turn Off Your Lights:
http://goo.gl/3DXNn

Earth Hour:
http://goo.gl/wCYfL

31

To the Kinder,

As the days get longer in the spring, my humans turn off the big blasty hot air thingy. Most nights I am just fine with this decision. It has been chilly only a few times since they have done this, but no worries for me as I have ample furriness. See my back paw?

I have also observed them moving the number dial thingy up and down all winter. It seems they are through with this, at least for a while. I think this must be a smart human move. Besides when it gets a little chilly, we just all curl up together. The Big One has very warm feet. Stay cozy!

Luff, Gizmo

What about us humans?

For every single degree that you can lower your thermostat, a saving of about 3% per day accumulates. Installing a programmable thermostat will take care of remembering to make adjustments and, on top of it, will result in more savings. When the summer months of air conditioning are upon us consider turning the dial up at night.

Although Gizmo does not like it, close the drapes and blinds on hot sunny days. All of these measures practiced together are common sense moves that mean less energy used and more savings.

Alright, let's really do something . . .

Adults – Have an energy audit done to see where your home heating or cooling lacks efficiency and address these areas. If you need monetary assistance, it might be available through your energy provider. Persist and get it done. Install a programmable thermostat or program yourself to adjust the settings.

Kids – Don't complain. If it is too hot, change into something cooler. If it is too cold, put on an extra shirt or a pair of socks. (You get the drift?) Try thinking about the opposite to what you are feeling . . . the arctic in summer or the desert in the winter.

Together – Conserve, conserve, conserve. As we heard growing up, "We are not heating the neighborhood, close the door!"

For more info . . .

Home Energy Audit:
http://goo.gl/xH1uC
http://goo.gl/w0zVc

Energy Efficiency Tips For Kids:
http://goo.gl/AI8hr

DIY Energy Audits:
http://goo.gl/WGf5h

greetings, Moppets,

That's me taking a snooze after eating
my lunch. I can eat the contents of
my bowl right down to the nubbins.
My humans are right there to fill it up
and also give me fresh water.

I get a fresh, sparkling bowl of water
a few times every day. When the Lady
changes my water, she uses the old water

to give drinks to all the green plants around here. There are a lot of them. From my height,

it is
like a jungle.
Sometimes she gets a puzzled look on her face. I think she is trying to figure out what part of the jungle to give a drink to.

This must be a smart human move as our jungle seems very thick and lush. Well I'm full now. Time for a cat nap.

Luff, Gizmo

What about us humans?

So called "waste water" is very plentiful around our homes these days. Try watering your plants with leftover water from cooking dinner or from the pet's water dish. If you keep a few plants that need humidity, try a naturally humid spot like over the kitchen sink or by a shower. Another good rule of thumb is to turn the faucet water on so that it runs out in a stream about the size of a pencil. We rarely need the force of a fully open faucet and this really saves on the amount of water used. When we become more aware of the water we use, we are using common sense for common good.

Alright, let's really do something . . .

Adults – Install a rain barrel or some type of catchment system outdoors. Water the garden and outside plants with water that has been conserved. Do the same thing in your kitchen on a miniature level with a bucket under the sink for pasta water or boiled egg water etc. Don't send it down the drain–use it.

Kids – Make sure you drink enough good clean water every day. Take care of the animals in your life and provide the same for them, especially when it's hot.

Together – Try carrying a gallon or two of water for a walk around the block. Now imagine what it would be like to walk a few miles with many more gallons placed in a container that you balance on your head. Find out where on this planet they do this and why.

For more info . . .

8 Signs You Are Wasting Water:
http://goo.gl/yMaF7

Water Quiz:
http://goo.gl/DbPYw

39

Hi, Rascals,

My humans sometimes come back from being away with all these reusable bags filled with stuff.

As I watch them unpack the bags, I look for the stuff I like. Turns out, I am very fond of the orange colored things they bring back to our house. My three recent favorites are mangos, carrots, and cheese. But, mostly, I just like it when the bags are empty and I get to hide in them. They are filled with all kinds of great smells and I just love to roll around inside and get those smells all up in my fur.

Here is another one of those smart human moves. They reuse the bags. I hope they bring 'em back in the house again real soon full of some more great smelly stuff.

Luff, Gizmo

PULL HANDLES UP
NOT OUT

Really bad move
Chris—this bag is
paper—you need new
glasses.

**Price
CUT**

Every aisle.

What about us humans?

Gizmo likes the smells that are left in the reusable bag, smells left by organic produce not packaged in cartons or plastic. Try to avoid using the plastic bags provided at the store for your produce. There are natural, washable alternatives, so skip the bags at the store altogether. Get used to carrying your own reusable shopping bags and produce bags. Those netted bags work great for fruits and veggies. Once you have started this common sense habit, it is an easy one to maintain. Just keep a supply handy, maybe stashed in your vehicle, and you will always be prepared for any shopping excursion. We can answer the question "Paper or plastic?" with "no thanks, brought my own!"

Alright, let's really do something . . .

Adults – Always carry your own bags and refillable containers for everything. Decline any and all bags offered. Banish plastic bags from your life. Help banish them from your town or city with legislation. Contact your representative.

Kids – When you carry your own lunch, use a reusable bag or metal lunch box. Help at the grocery store by packing the reusable bags and then at home by unpacking the groceries. Refold the reusable bags for their next use. Put them where you will always remember to take them along.

Together – Offer a friend a reusable bag. Help spread the good habit to everyone you know.

For more info . . .

Reuse:
http://goo.gl/nIZu0

Reusable bags:
http://goo.gl/oE0U9

43

My precious Wee Ones,

Ahhhhhhh, those morning smells. I know my humans are up and at 'em when I smell that yummy thick woodsy smell. They make that smell using a machine in the kitchen near my food and water bowl.

The Big One, who usually makes the stuff, puts some very dark brown speckles into the machine and then adds some water. They have to change out the speckles every day. They put the old speckles in a bowl and I see them take them outside and put them in the garden.

I like this time in the morning because I also get fresh water and food. This must be another one of those smart human moves, like not wasting the water. They are not wasting the speckles. The plants in the garden seem to like the speckles as much as my humans.

Luff, Gizmo

What about us humans?

Composting our waste is another way to make use of the embodied energy of plant sources. Many kinds of waste can be added directly to a garden. For the rest try composting. By some estimates, about one third of our trash could be composted. This would save a great deal of landfill space and also provide vital soil nutrition. Most home improvement stores and garden centers have the simple equipment needed to begin this backyard practice. Also, try a small compost unit under the sink. Once you establish the practice of composting, the habit is an easy one to maintain and very good for the planet. Composting is a common sense for common good step we can all take.

Alright, let's really do something . . .

Adults – Start a neighborhood or building compost site. Use the nutritious soil produced to begin gardens in your backyards or in patio pots. Grow something.

Kids – Start a compost program at your school. Find out where your lunch waste can go so that it can be recycled back into good nutritious soil instead of being dumped into landfills.

Together – Share what you have grown in your garden with someone else.

For more info . . .

Composting:
http://goo.gl/BtDQk

How to Compost:
http://goo.gl/ZvAXR

Growing Power:
http://goo.gl/XDAzz

(rewrite this mess)

Lighting Needs

- replace ~~8~~, ~~&~~ 7 leds watt for
  40 watt CFL (or lower)

- remove $\frac{+4}{=11}$
  3 - lower level
      ceiling fixture)
  2 - each bathroom (above shower)
      = (replace)

- check out
  CFL ??
  for lamps w/ harps
                  × 3

[recycle (×4)]

need this →
shape to
fit —

[3 ways ??]

✓ CFL / LED nightlights ? ask?

48

Hi, Rug Rats,

OBSERVATION
11

I am exhausted. I have been doing intellectrical work all day with my humans. They have been going room to room, looking at all the lights in every room. With paper and pencil in hand, they have been taking notes about all those lights in every nook and cranny of this place.

Some of our lights are big ones and some are tiny, like the light near my private box. Some of our lights are all curled up like a snake and some of them are very, very sparkly, like the one near the bowl I like to snooze in. I think all of this intellectrical observation is building up to another one of those smart human moves.

I will let you know what happens with all this.

Luff, Gizmo

What about us humans?

Taking stock of your household lighting efficiency is one way to cut back on energy use. Examine the lighting in your home. Can some or all of the bulbs be replaced with CFL or LED lighting sources? The added expense of purchasing these bulbs to replace traditional types can be planned out and accomplished over time. Just make an inventory of what you need and then watch for sales at stores near you, or online. Over the long term, the savings will add up and the costs of replacement offset by these savings. Replacing older bulbs with more efficient ones is a common sense for common good move that is good for our budgets and good for our planet.

Now _this_ is a modern light bulb. Welcome to the 21st century, Chris.

Alright, let's really do something . . .

Adults – Loosen and/or remove light bulbs where they are in multiples and one will do just fine, like ceiling fixtures and the garage door opener. Be very careful that little fingers will never have access to any open sockets. Then, going forward, when bulbs fail replace them with CFL or LED types.

Kids – If you know of places where the light is too bright (or too dim), let an adult know and help them put the right amount of light where it is needed.

Together – Discover why a traditional light bulb uses more energy than the newer types like CFL or LED. Learn about how electricity generates heat and why CFL or LED bulbs are more efficient users of energy.

For more info . . .

Energy Efficient Lighting:
http://goo.gl/pThDX

Energysavers
http://goo.gl/wpYQs

Hey, Nippers,

There is a lot to be said for the great outdoors. To feel the wind through your whiskers and smell the smells of the world is a little bit of heaven on Earth.

I especially like being up close and personal with my bird friends. Usually I only get to see them through the giant screen, but when I move past this barrier into their world, well, it's my own version of high-definition. My humans really enjoy this spot, too.

I think being right out in Mother Nature must be another one of those smart human moves. I never want to come in when they say I should. I play their treat game when they call me in by shaking the bag. Just don't tell 'em I know what they are doing.

Luff, Gizmo

What about us humans?

It is said that to appreciate and value nature one must spend time experiencing it. Whether that is the backyard, as it is for Gizmo, or the mountain tops or the depths of the ocean, we touch a common connecting thread among us when we connect with Earth. Maybe we would appreciate this gift of Mother Nature if we spent more time with her. Maybe we would take care of her better if we valued her more. The next time you are in a position to take off your shoes and feel the sand between your toes, or the grass beneath your soles, or the water rush over your feet. Try it. You might just discover a connection of common good . . . the planet we all inhabit.

Alright, let's really do something . . .

Adults – Harken back to a time when you connected with nature. Think back to the sensory experience. What did you see, smell, hear, and feel? Set aside some time to spend with nature.

Kids – Find a comfortable safe spot and watch the clouds float by, listen to the wind in the trees, or smell the flowers in a garden. Imagine yourself on a mountain top or floating down a river. How do you feel?

Together – Make nature a priority experience. Plan a walk or a trip to a park. Reconnect on a regular basis with that which connects us all – Mother Earth.

For more info . . .

Wilderness Adventures:
http://goo.gl/20gqm

Enjoying Mother Nature:
http://goo.gl/qNPVg

Dear Kittens,

When my humans are going out for the day, they sometimes pack a lunch.

A human lunch, I have learned, is a couple of brown squares with some stuff in the middle. The stuff varies from tuna (which I love and usually get a taste of) to cheese, to some brown sticky gooey stuff, to some more stuff which I do not know. They wrap up their lunch in some crinkly paper and put it in a bag that they reuse over and over again.

Sometimes I get to play with the paper when they come home. I like to bat it around and feel it crunch under my paws. This must be a smart human move — this lunch thing.

Luff, Gizmo

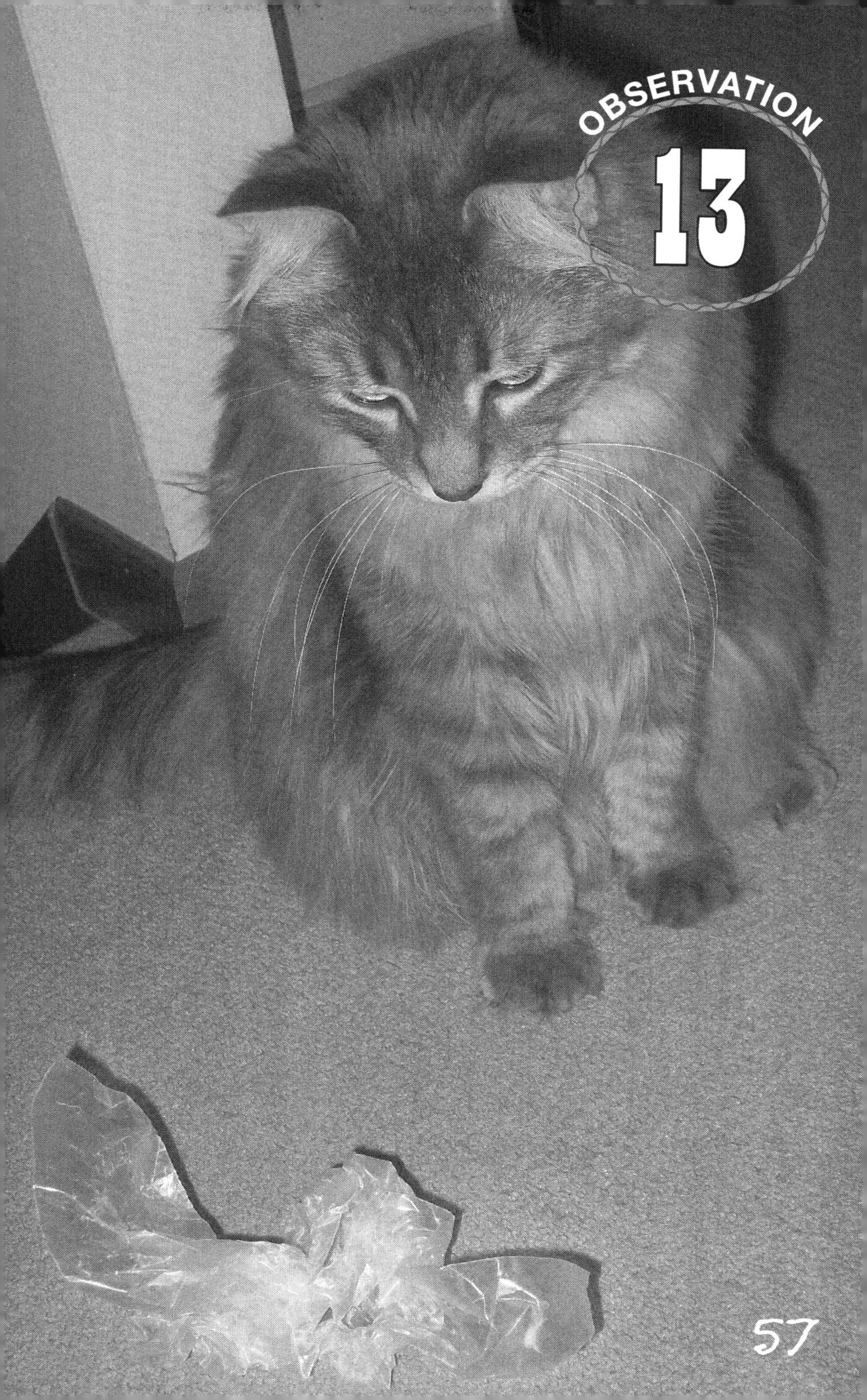
OBSERVATION
13

What about us humans?

Gizmo's humans are using wax paper to wrap up their sandwiches. This is a common sense move as wax paper is generally more earth friendly than plastic. Look for wax paper bags, too. The non-petroleum based wax paper is ultimately the best choice, but any alternative that keeps plastic out of our landfills and our oceans makes good common sense.

We need to have a serious conversation with ourselves about the notion of convenience and what it is doing to the planet and each other. So much of what we throw away falls into the plastic/garbage category that these two words have come to mean about the same.

Plastic (except for the bio version) is a petroleum-based product that is virtually indestructible and certainly not biodegradable.

Think seriously about how much of your eating is somehow linked to plastic and how bad this is for you, let alone the planet.

Alright, let's really do something . . .

Adults – Remove all plastic wrap from your life and the lives of those you live with. Ask an older person how they lived without plastic and adopt some of these ways as your own.

Kids – Discover how plastic is made and what happens to it in a landfill. Try burying a plastic plate and a paper plate and then digging them up after a year.

Together – Pack eco-friendly lunches together for school and for work.

For more info . . .

Plastic Wrap Alternatives:
http://goo.gl/pobrS

Eco-Friendly Lunch:
http://goo.gl/Fhdhl

Cherubs,

My humans are rustlin' up some grub.

The Lady is getting out the pointy silver sticks, the cloths, and the big round circles. Boy, oh boy, they have a lot of things they have to eat with. They use the pointy silver sticks to put the food in their mouths and the cloths to wipe it off when they miss their mouths.

Me, I munch some bits of snipples and then take a quick wet paw to my mouth and I am done with the clean up.

That's me as a kitten, wasn't I sweet?!

These humans wash the big round circles and the pointy silver sticks in the sink by my food dish and the cloths in the big white box in the basement. They reuse everything.

This must be another one of their smart human moves. I think I am smarter though. All I use is my mouth and my paw.

Luff, Gizmo

61

What about us humans?

Making the move to a totally reusable dinner table may mean ditching the paper plates, the plastic forks, and the paper napkins. If you have gotten used to eating with disposables, make the gradual shift to all reusables. It really *is* easier and makes for a more pleasant dining experience. You don't have to keep buying the stuff only to throw it away! Look for cloth napkins at garage or tag sales or make some of your own out of scrap fabric. Some folks even use kitchen towels for everyday cloth napkins. A different one for each diner in your house means they can be washed only when they need to be and this saves water, too. Common sense dining means trying to throw out as little as possible.

Alright, let's really do something . . .

Adults – Ban disposables from your eating experiences at home. If you buy take-out, pass on the plastic ware and paper napkins.

Kids – Help wash dishes and clean up after meal time. Sing songs, dance or talk about good books to read. (Like mine 🐾!!)

Together – Make meals more enjoyable with shared responsibilities and shared rewards. Look someone in the eye while you try to balance those peas on your fork. Reconnect with each other and help the planet, too.

For more info . . .

Waste and Recycling Facts:
http://goo.gl/B6yFL

The Zero Waste Home:
http://goo.gl/zlJ6d

action in "Dark of the Moon" is clear and it doesn't feel like an assault because it's broken up with humor, a smidge of romance and even a little mystery. In other words, this is exactly what a summer movie should be.

Chris Hewitt can be reached at 651-228-5552.

"TRANSFORMERS: DARK OF THE MOON"
Directed by: Michael Bay
Starring: Shia LaBeouf, Rose Huntington-Whiteley
Rated: PG-13 for nonstop violence, brief, strong language and sex talk
Should you go? Yes. Load up on the popcorn and enjoy. ★★★½

the lizards

Theater

Minnetonka teen wins national theater award

A teenager from Minnesota and one from New York won top honors at the National High School Musical Theater Awards on Monday night, sweeping to glory by mastering "Glee"-type competition by mastering songs by Stephen Sondheim and Frank Loesser.

Ryan McCartan, from Minnetonka,

You Scallywags,

I am trying to figure out why my humans like to look at this so much.
They laugh as they look at it and they spend time talking to each other about what is on it. I think it is something that only humans can understand, but I am going to try to crack the code.

Even the guys in the green trash truck like this thing. They come by every week to pick them up. I can spy 'em out of my upstairs lookout post. This must be important to a lot of humans, 'cuz the guys in the green truck pick these things up from practically every house I can see.

When I figure out what this is, I will let you know. Gizmo is on the case.

Luff, Gizmo

What about us humans?

Even Gizmo's litter is made of recycled materials. There really is no excuse not to recycle these days. If you are not sure where to recycle your paper, call your waste management service or local government offices and ask them if they have a collection program. If you do not have a paper recycling program at work, get one started. It is just as easy to throw the paper in the recycling bin as it is to throw it in the trash. This is a move that is good for the bottom line, and boy it is good for the trees!

Alright, let's really do something . . .

Adults – Read your news online. Communicate by email, text, twitter, or electronic alternative. Print on paper only when necessary. Buy and use recycled paper products only. Recycle all paper.

Kids – Make sure the paper used in your classroom is recycled. Set up a school program. Collect newspapers, recycle them and donate the proceeds to planting trees.

Together – Plant enough trees to offset your family's paper use for a year. How many would it take? Do the research.

For more info . . .

Paper Recycling:
http://goo.gl/zcDpp

Cat Litter:
http://goo.gl/5BVAg

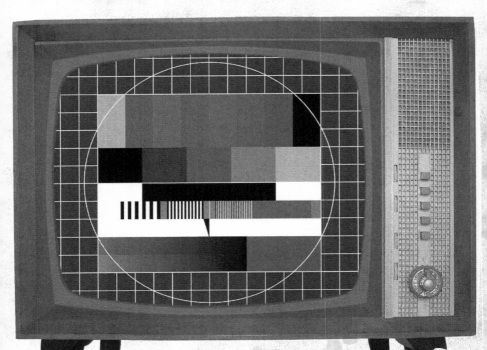

My Dear Pups,

Seems the TeeVahDee
is on its way out. The
Big One says it is done
being fixed and past its
prime. They are going
to recycle the poor old thing
says the Lady. Am I supposed to
be sad for the TeeVahDee? I hope the
recycle place it is going to is as nice
as our home.

Luff, Gizmo

This letter is short and sweet to leave space for a big beautiful picture of ME!! Dig the pose?

What about us humans?

From batteries to cell phones to light bulbs to televisions, properly dispose of equipment by recycling or donating. Gone are the days of dumping these items in the landfill. Now we know too much about what the contents of these items can do to the planet if not treated properly. Be responsible! Find a good home for all the equipment you no longer use. And think about using items until they wear out before you replace them. New is good. Just know exactly what you are going to do with the old before replacing it.

Alright, let's really do something . . .

Adults – Ask yourself do I really *need* to replace this cell phone, TV, computer? If you do, find a place for the old one first. Consider donating the item if you can afford the purchase of a new one.

Kids – Take care of the things in your life. Try to make them last.

Together – Learn where an item like a TV goes once it is recycled. What happens to all the parts?

For more info . . .

Recycling:
http://goo.gl/2HvOX

Computer Recycling:
http://goo.gl/jeS9H

Energy Star and TVs:
http://goo.gl/pBp8Q

Bambinos,

I am very aware that my humans are feeding me a kind of food they think is good for me. The labels on the packages say things like "all natural" and "organic." All I really care about is that the food is tasty. And, as long as I do their requested tricks, like "sit," I get my treats, too.

Sometimes I just go and sit by the place where they keep the treats. I am trying to

What no picture of me? Oh there I am. Chris why am I so small, what is this mess?

train them, too. I especially like the treats they say have vitamins in them. They are, indeed, tasty. Whether it is my food or my treats, vitimazation seems important to them. What makes my humans happy makes me happy.

Luff, Gizmo

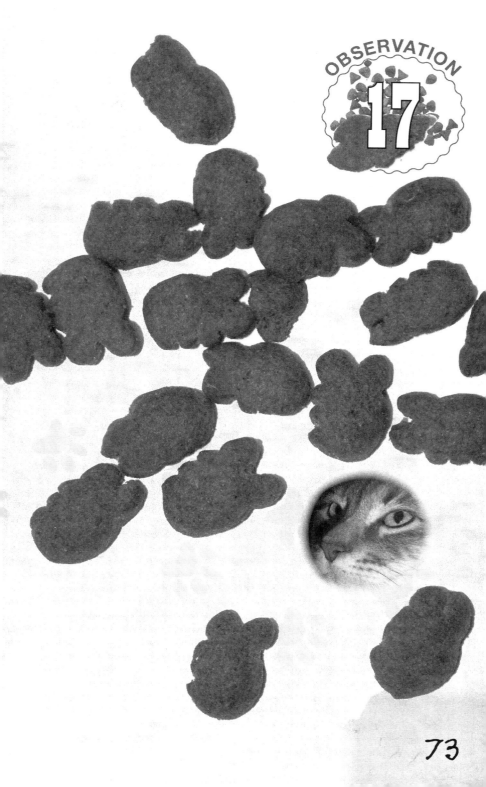

What about us humans?

Globally, many food products are labeled as natural or organic these days. Generally, organic foods are grown without the use of chemical-based fertilizers or synthetic-based pesticides. Look for the organic label on food products worldwide. Try to buy organic if possible. For us and for our pet friends, finding the best, healthiest, and least environmentally toxic food source is good for them, us, and the planet.

Alright, let's really do something . . .

Adults – Educate yourself regarding organic and non-organic fruits and veggies. You may be very surprised which fruits and veggies are heavily laden with pesticides if not grown organically. Try to purchase organic options – or grow them yourself.

Kids – Eat your broccoli and try to enjoy it. Smile, it is good for you, and the adult who prepared it wants you to be healthy.

Together – Shop for produce together and explore some new fruit and vegetable options. Look for organic labeling and learn to recognize it.

For more info . . .

Organic Foods, Safer/More Nutritious:
http://goo.gl/glWMr

Organic vs Nonorganic:
http://goo.gl/rkfYK

oooh aaaah!

Our Nestlings,

OBSERVATION
18

The Big One has a chunk of the backyard he likes to play in. I can see him digging in this play box and putting stuff in the ground. Some of the stuff he has stuck in the ground has gotten very big and bushy.

He likes this piece of the backyard, I know, because he spends a good deal of time in it. I can watch him from my second-story lookout post while he plays. Lately when he is done playing, he brings in some of the stuff that is in his backyard play box. The Lady makes "oooooo" and "aaaaaaah" sounds, so I know this stuff makes her happy, too.

On the next page is a picture of one of the things he has in his play box.

Luff, Gizmo

What about us humans?

Spring, summer, and fall are the times of the year
where our backyard gardens really start to bear the
fruits of our labor. So much produce is in season
throughout these times it makes it difficult to choose
what to eat first. If you do not have a garden, you can
visit a farmer's market or local grower. Becoming a
member of a CSA (community supported agriculture)
group is also a way to get local produce when it is in
season. If you have a garden of bounty, try to think
of ways to share this with those not in a position to
grow their own produce or simply in need of food for
survival. This is a common sense for common good
idea that could change the world.

Alright, let's really do something . . .

Adults – Plant and harvest. Share this experience with a young person. Teach the next generation the joys of gardening and just plain playing in the dirt. We all need to know where real food comes from and what it looks like.

Kids – Plant and harvest. Share this experience with an adult. Learn about and grow a food you have never tried before. Expand your food horizons.

Together – Share the harvest. Connect with your neighbors through the bounty of the planet. Help feed each other.

For more info . . .

Shop Local:
http://goo.gl/wn143

Backyard Gardening:
http://goo.gl/KfQsB

Gizzy's Friends,

I am going to let you in on a little secret. My Lady gives me paw massages.

You see, my paws have some toes and a very big pad that really like it when she stretches them out and rubs them. I think this is called felinexology and she is very good at it. She sometimes does this to the Big One, too. His paws are much bigger than mine and seem furless on the bottom.

All I know is that it is relaxing and I feel better after. I have happy feet. She smiles, too.

Luff, Gizmo

Don't worry, Chris didn't lay all that food out, he says this is Abstract Paw Art and finds it funny. Oh dear!

What about us humans?

We know the foot, or paw, is connected to everything—in many ways. Our feet, and Gizmo's paws, can really bear the brunt of a hurried existence. Common sense means also paying attention to our health and relieving the stress of our day-to-day existence. Foot massage, or reflexology, can increase circulation. This is believed to help with overall stress from the tip of our heads to our toes. Connecting with each other, whether we are human or feline, is a step toward a sense of common good. Happiness is a planetary goal we can all appreciate. When Gizmo is happy, so are we.

Apparently this is how some Chinese people write the word happiness!!! Or is Chris pulling my paw?

Alright, let's really do something . . .

Adults – Learn about reflexology. Try a foot massage. If you are unable to massage your own feet, enlist a buddy or just try rolling the bottom of your feet over a bumpy surface.

Kids – Watch a cat when they first get up from a nap and stretch. If you are feeling tense or tired, try a stretch or two, like Gizmo. Pay attention to your own health and make healthy choices for your life.

Together – How can we help each other deal with day-to-day stress? Help your buddy, whether animal or human, and help yourself with healthy actions that relieve stress and promote a sense of happiness.

For more info . . .

Free Reflexology:
http://goo.gl/8VpAi

Stress Management:
http://goo.gl/PgFt2

84

Hi, Youngsters,

It has been so hot around here lately. One day it was over a million degees. Nope, sorry, a hundred.

What's a degee?

The Big One took a silver stick to the tires on his car to check something he called pressure. Then the Lady asked him to do the same thing to her car.

They are trying to get "decent mileage" says the Big One. The Big One had to let some air out of all of his tires and two of the tires on the Lady's car.

I am going back inside, too many degees out here.

Luff, Gizmo

Check out the next page. I think Chris was getting tired of my picture in every entry. What is that thing!

What about us humans?

Gizmo keenly observed his humans adjusting the air pressure in their vehicle tires. Something that motoring experts say we all need to pay more attention to, in order to get better mileage. Better mileage is a win-win for our pocketbooks and the planet. Less fuel burned is a common sense for common good practice we can all embrace. And a well maintained car is a car that reduces its impact on the environment and potentially stays on the road longer.

Alright, let's really do something . . .

Adults – Do the regular maintenance your vehicle requires, including tire pressure checks. Get a pressure gauge so you can do this yourself. Find a location nearby that has free air and check it regularly, especially if you live in a climate where the temperatures vary up and down considerably.

Kids – If you have a bike, learn about tire air pressure. If you don't have a bike, learn anyway because someday you may have a car. Fill a balloon with air and put it in the freezer. Check it after two hours. What happened? Why?

Together – Take the car in for servicing. Learn that machines need care and maintenance to run well.

For more info . . .

Tire (UK Tyre) Pressure:
http://goo.gl/FWsIH

Greening Your Road Trip:
http://goo.gl/oK5Gw

Dear Tots,

The Lady cleans her big sink and my cool round bowl with a great smelling fruity spray. She squirts it into her sink and my bowl. Then a few minutes later she scrubs them clean.

She says she is not worried about me being around when she is doing this because the spray is not going to hurt me. The Lady is so careful that I am taken care of. I could tell you what is

Chris looked for pictures of smells, but no luck. I know what a smell looks like, but apparently photographers aren't so clever!

in this spray, but I am not sure about the ingedients.

I will ask her to tell you about the ingedients so you can make some yourself.

Luff, Gizmo

What about us humans?

Many non-toxic cleaners are available today on store shelves or you can mix your own. Here is an easy recipe, which is also a cheap alternative. Take a clean, empty, quart- or litre-sized spray bottle (use a safe type of plastic one) and fill it (not quite) with one-half white vinegar and one-half water. Leave some space at the top. Add about a ¼ cup of environmentally friendly dish soap to the bottle. If you like, add a few drops of an essential oil like orange, lavender, or lemon. Gently mix. Spray and wipe clean. If you have a grimy sink or tub, scrub it first with baking soda and a little water. This practice is good because no harsh chemicals end up going down the drain or are inhaled.

Alright, let's really do something . . .

Adults – Do not use toxic cleaners. Educate yourself about what ingredients are toxic and remove them from your home. If you do not want to spend the time learning about all the chemicals that are toxic, purchase products from reputable companies that are toxic free.

Kids – Never use a cleaning-type product unless supervised by an adult. Know what you are using. Use only safe products. Learn some basic chemistry. Try cleaning with baking soda paste and vinegar spray. Watch what happens. Why?

Together – Make cleaning together fun by using safe products that everyone can use without the fear of harmful effects.

For more info . . .

GoodGuide:
http://goo.gl/0uAAY

Green Cleaning:
http://goo.gl/kZmeu

Hola, Offspring,

Happy Birthday to me, Happy Birthday to me, Happy Birthday, dear Gizmo Smiley Olson Johnson a.k.a. Killer, the Don, Poncho, praying kitty, Mr. Otter, kitchen police, supe, lion heart, Bose boy, Mr. Clean, mo man, fine chap, mas' Joe, Renfield, winky winky, spooknik, Frigidaire, nurse gizmo, Mr. Curious, lover boy, and Gizzy... Happy Birthday to me.

I was born on 9/9/09. I was bottle fed from the time I was born for my cat mom did not feed me, my human moms did. So, sing me a happy birthday song. If you want, I'll save you a piece of cake. Better hurry or you can fuggetabowtit!

Luff, Gizmo

What about us humans?

Gizmo's birthday is an important reminder of how connected all of life is. Had he not been supported in his earliest days, he would not be around to remind us all how to live more sustainable lives. His humans, also, would have a hard time imagining life without him. Recognition of the interconnectedness of life can be a fundamental step toward embracing what is sustainable for all living things on the planet. How we treat other living things is ultimately how we treat ourselves.

Alright, let's really do something . . .

Adults – If you have any kids, make this planet a safe and healthy place for them to live.

Kids – If you have any pets, make this planet a safe and healthy place for them to live.

Together – If you have a planet, make it a safe and healthy place for all to live.

For more info . . .

Earth Institute:
http://goo.gl/mb1hP

Planet Health:
http://goo.gl/Hq07a

My Wonderful Neighbors,

See my toy store? My granny made me this banky when I was a baby, and now I use it to display my huge collection of toys. I don't really need all of these and, if you came over, I would give you whatever you want from the selection. Well, maybe not whatever you want. I have a couple of favorites. Ah, never mind, if you want it, you can have it. There's more where they came from.

Like the sign says, "Gizmo's toy store, c'mon in and browse."

Call for daily hours of operation or by appointment.

Luff, Gizmo

What about us humans?

The piles and piles of stuff that clog our lives have to have some purpose beyond just creating more piles. A real step toward sustainable living would be to think twice before you buy. We live with way too much stuff; stuff that could be used by someone else or used to create income needed to support others. Take a look around. Can the unused stuff of your life find a home with someone who needs it or a charity that can sell it to help someone out? Stop spending so much time taking care of stuff. Take care of someone (or some living thing) instead. This is a common sense for common good move.

Alright, let's really do something . . .

Adults – Think before you buy. Pare down and give away. Remember the questions to ask yourself: 1. Do I need it? 2. Do I use it regularly? 3. Could someone else use it?

Kids – If you are running out of space and your room is getting a bit overrun with stuff, well that is a sign. Ask yourself what is the difference between need and want?

Together – The next time you feel a need to shop for _____ (fill in the blank with a non-essential), shop instead for someone else's need. Ask yourselves, a few weeks after, if you really miss not getting the _____ (fill in the blank), you felt you HAD to have. Learn about the cycle of stuff detailed in the book and on the web site called "The Story of Stuff" (see below) and make an effort to alter this cycle of stuff in your own life. Ask yourselves, " Why is there seemingly always more where that came from?"

For more info . . .

The Story of Stuff:
http://goo.gl/uGW0c

Our Hopes,

Boy, it gets chilly at night now.

My humans have been putting on different kinds of clothes and now they cover up at night with their bankys. Good thing I have all this fur. The Big One took a look up the chimney where I can hear the wind and sometimes hear my loud-mouth bird friends. MMMMMM, he said, it might need cleaning. Then he checked the big blasty hot air thingy downstairs. It has some kind of flat paper stiff thingy that they do not want to get dirty. The Big One was holding it up to the light. It looked pretty disgustapating. He told the Lady to get a new one before the snow flies.

I didn't know that snow could fly. I will examine it more closely when it comes. Does it have wings?

Luff, Gizmo

This is a dirty
filter of some sort
that Chris got all
excited about. I just
can't control him!

What about us humans?

When colder months approach, it is time to think about the heat we will need in our homes. Changing the air filter is an important way to keep a furnace (or for that matter an air conditioner) operating as efficiently as possible. Look at the filter at least once a month. This is particularly important if you have animals in the house, live in the town, or if anyone in the home has allergies or breathing problems. Cleaning wood-burning fixtures like stoves and fireplaces is important for efficiency and safety. If your heat is delivered through radiators, check for leaks and think about installing individual unit controls so heat can be delivered to the areas most in use. Every little bit helps in creating a more energy efficient home.

Alright, let's really do something . . .

Adults – Besides changing the furnace/AC filter, get the unit inspected and serviced or consider replacing it with an energy efficient model. The same goes for the fireplace, the wood burning stove, or the radiators. Regular servicing of whatever type of heat source you use, can extend the life of equipment and delay costly total replacement. All of our sources of heat, when running efficiently, save energy and money.

Kids – Learn the laws of layering your clothing. Many layers will keep you warmer. As you warm up, peel the layers off. Also, don't run around the house in the middle of the winter in bare feet and complain about the cold, and don't run around the house in the summer with your boots on . . . get it? Dress intelligently with the weather in mind. How does a bear dress for winter? What does a reptile do when it is hot?

Together – Live a little cooler in the winter and a little hotter in the summer. Learn to adjust like our furry friends who shed in the warm weather and put on another layer of fur in the cold weather. Think of natural and fun ways to cool off and/or stay warm.

For more info . . .

Furnace Filters:
http://goo.gl/UyFNT

Keeping Cool in the Heat:
http://goo.gl/6xirC

Precious Ones,

Remember, what I told you about last week, well, the snow has stared to fly and I am going to have to get a big ol' pair of magnifier glasses 'cuz I can't see the wings. Maybe it has invincable wings? Anyway, my humans close the windows when they run the big blasty hot air thingy that heats up this joint. I am not very happy when my humans close the windows, but they say it is because they are not heating the neighborhood.

The Lady has this wonderful fruity spray she sprays after cooking the Big One's dinner. And she has another, more flowery one she uses in the bedroom. The Lady says these are all natural and they will not hurt me or the Big One. And, until she can open the windows again, the fruity flowers are the next best thing.

Luff, Gizmo

What about us humans?

Many of the sprays we use to "freshen" the air contain very harmful ingredients, especially for those with breathing conditions. If opening the windows to enhance outdoor and indoor air exchange is not wise, as in the coldest days of winter, use a natural—not chemically laden—air freshener spray. Also, essential oils, heated gently, will infuse the air with wonderfully aromatic scents. Or try the old-fashioned and simple method of heating a few spices in some water on the stove. Many natural and non-toxic ways exist to keep our air smelling fresh and, more importantly, safe to breathe and safe for the planet.

Alright, let's really do something . . .

Adults – A broken record plays again: If you don't know what the ingredients are, don't use it in your home, especially in a closed environment. Be particularly aware that some products contain ingredients linked to breathing problems.

Kids – Breathing really fresh air is good for you, so get outside and play when you can. But, heed adult warnings about air quality and stay indoors on days when the air is not safe to breathe.

Together – Keep on working for clean air in your community. Look into what programs are operating in your area and support their efforts. Volunteer to help.

For more info . . .

Air Pollution:
http://goo.gl/cJH79

Clean Air Act (USA):
http://goo.gl/TiQXI

Busy Beavers,

It's clean up day around here. Boy, these humans have a lot of equipment.

The Big One uses this noisy, wheeled, machine that sucks up my fur from the carpet. The Lady has some scrubby things for the floors, bath, the sinks and the reflection windows in the bathroom. They put their clothes in

the two white boxes and after some real busy time, wambo, it's done.

Me, I have all my equipment right with me. My scratchy tongue is the best for grabbing and smoothing. And, my paws, versatile if I do say so myself, get to every spot. I am a cleaning machine.

Luff, Gizmo

What about us humans?

Cleaning day at Gizmo's house is filled with eco-friendly products. From the laundry detergent to the bathroom mirror cleaner, environmentally friendly and non-toxic products are the way to a clean and healthy home for Gizmo and his humans. If you do not use these products yet, start with one area of cleaning, maybe the bathroom, and experience the difference. Natural smells will fill the air—not chemical smells—and what is being washed down the drains will not harm the environment. Common sense tells us it is not good to breathe the toxic fumes and common good tells us it is not wise to wash toxic products down our drains.

Alright, let's really do something . . .

Adults – Once and for all time, detoxify your life. All cleaning products we use on a daily or weekly or monthly basis should be totally non-toxic. Make the change in your home and share this cleaning information with someone else—your friends and family.

Kids – Help clean the house.

Together – Find out why it is important *never* to wash harmful chemicals down the drain. Research what these toxins do to the plant and animal life that come in contact with them. Find out why specific chemicals have been banned by certain countries in the world.

For more info . . .

EU Chemical Regulation:
http://goo.gl/yr1tw

Cleaning Recipes:
http://goo.gl/92Zhy

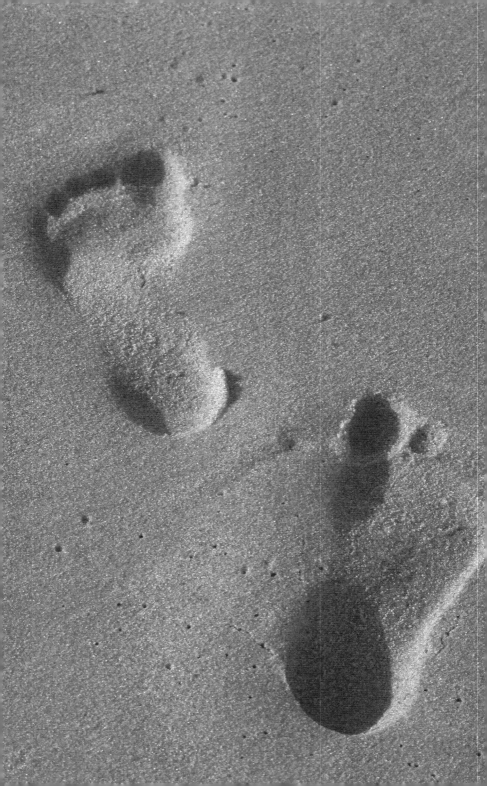

You want to come, too?

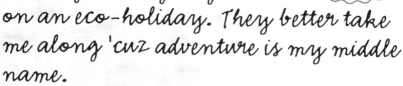

My humans have been talking about going on an eco-holiday. They better take me along 'cuz adventure is my middle name.

The Big One says to pack light, just some comfortable shoes and a couple of clothes changes for they have everything else we need where we are going. I don't wear clothes, and shoes? What are shoes?!

I am SO excited I can't stand it. I have to get some travel papers from my vet, Dr. Howe, so I can go along.

I will talk to you next week when we get where we are going. The Big One says it will be the trip of a lifetime.

Luff, Gizmo

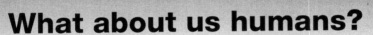

What about us humans?

Today, travel holds many options especially for those
environmentally inclined. Everything from staying
at an eco-friendly bed and breakfast to excursions
that take you half way around the world. If you want
to travel with the planet in mind, consider your
destination and the environmental impact of your
mode of transportation. Also, very simple items like
refillable containers and environmentally friendly soaps
will lessen the impact you have at wherever your
destination may be. A little bit of pre-planning can
make any trip less costly for the planet.

Alright, let's really do something . . .

Adults – Invest in a stainless steel water bottle (or some other safe version). Fill and then refill it on your trip even if your trip is just around the corner or up the street.

Kids – What part of the world would you like to experience? What animal do you want to see in its native habitat? Do some research and do some wishing!

Together – The next time you are packing for a trip pretend that you will have to bring everything back that you take, including the trash. Do you really want to carry that much stuff? Does it make sense to bring small containers that are refillable, not disposable? Plan and pack for your pretend trip with the planet in mind. What might you leave behind? What will you take with you?

For more info . . .

Eco Tours:
http://goo.gl/LfQCV

Calculate your carbon footprint:
http://goo.gl/zhY1t

115

Little Tykes,

We made it! The Lady packed my favorite banky with me on the plane and I was quite comfortable under the seat in my box. I slept most of the way.

We are staying in a hut in the woods out in the middle of a bunch of very big trees surrounded by smells and sounds like I never smelled or heard before. The Big One and the Lady sit on

the porch with their double big black
eye tubes and look out into the trees.
I think they are looking for those
things making all the noise. They say
that they want to see the noisemakers
in their natural world before they are
all gone.

Where are they going?

Luff, Gizmo

What about us humans?

Experiencing first-hand the wonders of nature is not an option open to all of us. If you can't get to see the rain forest like Gizmo, many online, print, and film options exist to experience the beauty of this planet. Try to get out of your world and into another part of this great planet and see for yourself the beauty and wonder of this earth we have. Scientists say we are losing so much of this world at such a rapid pace that the planet will not look the same for the generations that follow ours. What can you do to help the planet's survival?

Alright, let's really do something . . .

Adults – Figure out what part of your world you can help save and then do it. Fish conservation, wetlands preservation, save the whales . . . find the cause you resonate with and support it before it is too late.

Kids – Learn about a part of the planet you don't know too much about. Try the deepest parts of the ocean or the deserts of northern Africa or the innards of an ant hill. Become an educated part of the planet and what inhabits the planet we all share.

Together – Participate in Earth Day. Become active and help Earth.

For more info . . .

Kid's World Atlas:
http://goo.gl/zNQx9

Earth Day Network:
http://goo.gl/28vfX

Nature Conservancy:
http://goo.gl/CIVhd

Peace, Kids,

While in the hut, I have learned the art of meditation.

I clear my mind of all that is currently racing around in it and breathe very deeply. My thoughts can transport me to any place I choose. Sometimes I choose to think about the fish we had for dinner last night and how very tasty it was. Sometimes I think of my personal cable network channel I see at home and wonder how my bird friends are. Often, I think of nothing at all except the colors and shapes that float past my mind's eye.

It is no coinkidinky that I have learned to relax in the woods. I am hopeful I can do this at home, too.

Luff, Gizmo

121

What about us humans?

Gizmo is working on a skill that seems to come very naturally to cats. His ability to relax and take numerous catnaps at home reminds all of us that a busy life requires some rest and replenishment. As he has also stated, meditation is another form of this quiet relaxation and reflection time. Even a few deep breaths can help replenish us. Often, we humans wonder what is going through the minds of our animal friends. If only we could know. If only we could know.

Alright, let's really do something . . .

Adults – Clear the clutter out of your mind and make time to relax and meditate. Breathe deeply in through the nose and out through the mouth. Replenish, refresh, relax, reflect, and renew by practicing and perfecting life sustaining habits.

Kids – Discover how animals tell you what they are feeling. How do you know an animal is relaxed? How do you know that you are relaxed?

Together – Remember to breathe deeply.

For more info . . .

Meditation:
http://goo.gl/W5eTL

Meditation:
http://goo.gl/Weqik

Your Name is Mud,

My humans came back to the hut just covered with dirt and very sweaty. They said they were planting trees.

The Big One said they must have planted a few thousand in just one day. He said the other humans who were planting trees with them are also going home tomorrow.

The Lady filled a bucket with water and got out the good soap she brought from home. They are going to get cleaned up for dinner and then we head out tomorrow.

I will catch you on the flip side. Gizmo over and out.

Luff, Gizmo

What about us humans?

Trees are so very important to the overall health of this planet. Forests are natural carbon offsets as they absorb carbon dioxide and produce oxygen. Planting trees, especially as replacements for those lost to overdevelopment, is one of the important ways we can work to help the planet. If you are somehow responsible for the loss of trees, do your part and plant replacements. When we make the connection between our use of resource and the replenishment of that resource we are one more step toward lives of common sense for common good.

Alright, let's really do something . . .

Adults – Figure out how many trees you might plant to offset something you have planned, say a plane trip somewhere. Then, make this plane trip only if you are capable of offsetting your carbon production. Sounds harsh? When are we going to connect our use of resource with the replenishment of it?

Kids – Learn about tree planting programs, like Arbor Day. Plan a school project and follow through with planting trees.

Together – A family that plants together stays together. Plant a forest over your life time. What a legacy!

For more info . . .

Rainforest Alliance:
http://goo.gl/3Xi9V

Buy Trees:
http://goo.gl/tcteK

There's no place like Home Sweet Home!

I had so much fun on our trip. I do, however, like my regular food dishes and my regular box for my private duties.

Funny how it is always nice to get away but nice to get back home. I have missed my daily conversations with Sydney, my parrot buddy. He knows a lot about how things work and is very willing to share his wisdom with a little wipper snapper like me. Snowman (the white squirrel) is still messing around in the back yard, and the trees here still have a few leaves on them. They don't look anything like the leaves outside the hut, though.

My humans are checking the doors for some kind of strips as it has gotten colder around here. The Lady told the Big One they should have done this before we left—but better late than never. We are back at home base. Gizmo out.

Luff, Gizmo

129

What about us humans?

It is easy to lose track of the important energy saving things we can do to our homes especially in the light of epic adventure. Well, as the saying goes, it is never too late to make a good move. As the cold weather descends on all of us, checking the doors (and windows) for weather stripping is a pretty inexpensive and energy saving move to make. Try just placing a rolled up blanket or towel at the base of a door or along window ledges. This is a no cost move that can also lower the amount of heat lost through leaky doors and windows, if weather stripping is not in the budget. The common sense move of keeping the heat in the building is good for our budget bottom line.

Alright, let's really do something . . .

Adults – Check for leaks…fireplaces, doors, outlets, windows, attics, basements, cracks in the foundation, baseboards, vents, ducts, etc., and then address the leaks.

Kids – You can help install the weather stripping. You can also be a leak detective. Feel a cold draft? Where is it coming from?

Together – Help an elderly neighbor install some weather stripping. And, while you're at it, check to see if they need anything else done. Some day we will be in the same position as they are and be looking for a little kindness, too.

For more info . . .

Weather Stripping:
http://goo.gl/fnec5

Weather Stripping (UK):
http://goo.gl/oCvuY

132

Dear Ducklings,

My humans are bringing home less and less stuff in those bags I like to play in. Not so long ago, I can remember a few of them tossed on the floor for me to explore in. Now, it seems there are only one or two. And, those bags do not have so many other bags or boxes in them.

From what I can see from down here, when the bags are emptied out, my humans look like they have lots more real food and a whole lot less of that fancy wrapping. This makes sense to me. I wonder why it took them so long to figure out to just buy the food and not all the fancy wrapping.

Luff, Gizmo

What about us humans?

Gizmo is such a smart observer. He is speaking about a concept called *precycling*. This action is one in which you consider things such as processing, packaging, and waste for an item BEFORE you make the purchase. Can the food item be bought in a less processed, less packaged and less wasteful option?

Experts call this type of eating "slow food" as opposed to "fast food". Less processing and less packaging means less waste for the planet that we all share to asorb.

Alright, let's really do something . . .

Adults – Make meals at home from real ingredients. Involve kids in the entire process from picking out—or better yet, growing and harvesting—to preparing foods. Take the time to empower the next generation with respect for and skill with food preparation.

Kids – Imagine if everyone in your home ate a fast food meal once a week and that meal had a plastic fork, a napkin, wrapping—and it all came in a bag. All stuff that ends up in the trash. How many meals would that be? Now multiply that number times the number of kids in your class at school AND the number of classes in your school AND the number of schools in your town AND the number of towns near yours . . . do you understand?

Together – Be aware of packaging and extras (like plastic utensils) attached with eating "fast." Make some utensil packs for the car. A fork and spoon wrapped up in a cloth napkin. Better yet, try cooking at home!

For more info . . .

Precycling:
http://goo.gl/bv1oY

Recycling:
http://goo.gl/OP1RE

Math Garbage:
http://goo.gl/d1fik

My Beloveds,

This time of year seems so very strange to me. I have been watching the leaves float by my big viewing screen. Sometimes the wind takes them on such a ride, blowing them from one side of the screen to way off and out of my sight. And, when I place my paws on the edge of the screen, I now notice a chill.

I have successfully trained my humans to open the big screen and let me outside with just a simple meow or two. They are also trained to give me a treat when they call me back inside. This is the life.

I wonder where all the leaves fly off to? I will have to work on finding that out.

Luff, Gizmo

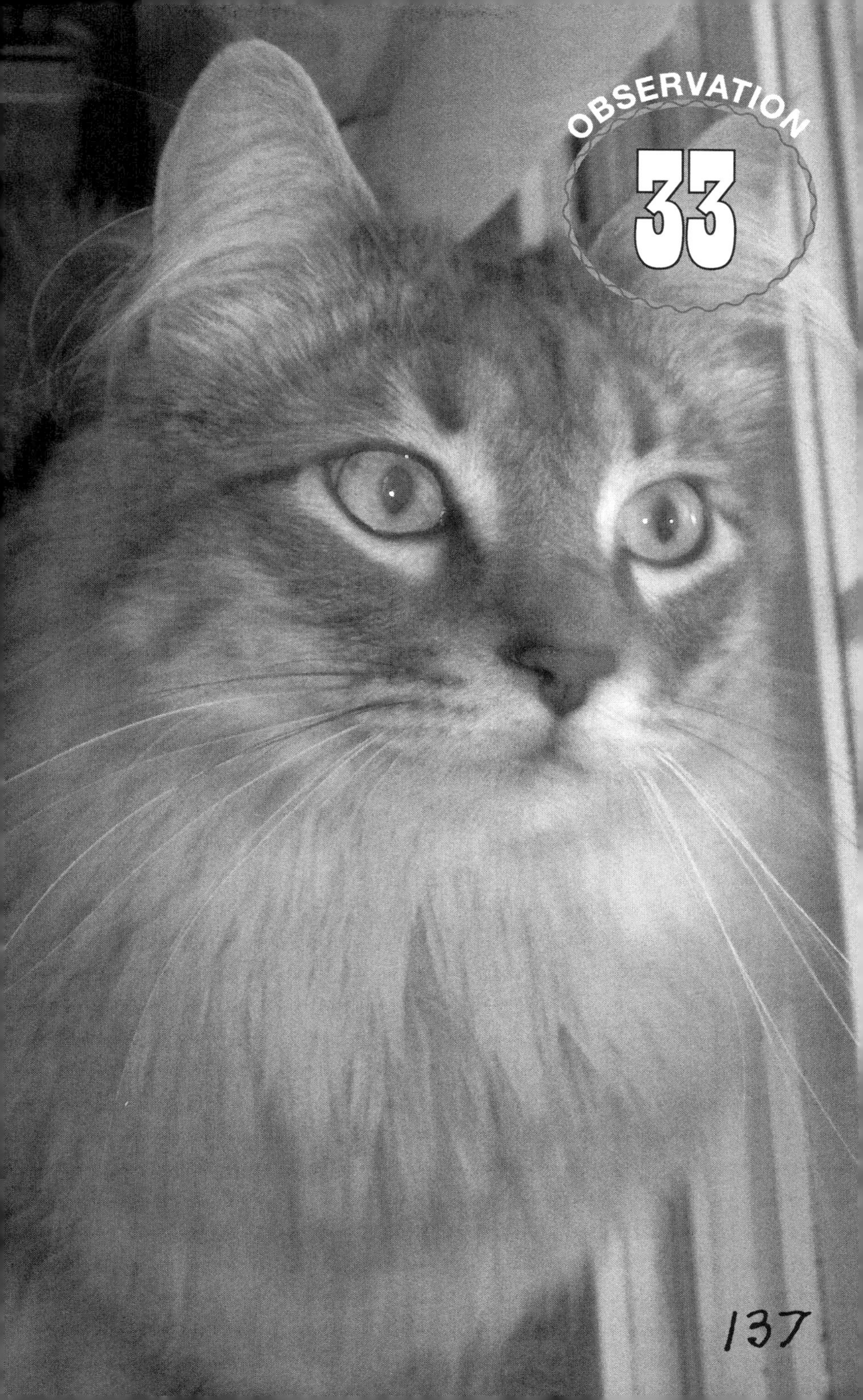

OBSERVATION 33

What about us humans?

Taking care of the leaves that have fallen off the trees in the autumn is one of many outdoor tasks in need of our attention. As we plant bulbs for next spring, rake leaves into piles, put away lawn furniture, and take care of all the rest of our outdoor jobs, please keep the planet in mind. For instance, putting leaves into plastic bags makes no sense. Because the leaves will decompose much more quickly than the plastic ever will, it is imperative that lawn clean-up be done with biodegradable bags. Most hardware and home improvement stores carry these bags for lawn and other uses. Or, try composting as another earth-friendly option. Starting a backyard compost pile is very easy. The resulting rich soil is good for the garden and ultimately the planet.

Alright, let's really do something . . .

Adults – Rethink the whole idea of garden waste. Don't use ordinary plastic bags for disposal. There are paper bags and biodegradable plastic-like bags for leaves. Nutrient rich yard waste can and should become our nutrient rich soil. Make some dirt.

Kids – Help rake some leaves and clean up some yards. Enlist your friends to do the same. Make a neighborhood leaf raking squad and spread the word you are available. Just be sure to use biodegradable and earth friendly bags.

Together – Remember, leaf piles have to be jumped in before they are removed from the yard.

For more info . . .

Composting:
http://goo.gl/IGHxK

Composting Leaves:
http://goo.gl/GlkQO

Sweetie Pies,

Ever since we got back from our trip my humans have been talking all about a  different kind of holiday. They say they want to give goats, water, eggs, seeds, and guinea pigs to all the folks on their list this year.

I think I know what a goat is. I get fresh water in my bowl a few times a day to drink. Eggs, I like 'em hard boiled, especially the bright yellow part. And seeds, I know I saw the Lady put some in the dirt a while back. But a guinea pig? What's a guinea pig? And what do you do with it once you know what it is?

I will have to get back to you on this one.

Luff, Gizmo

What about us humans?

When the holiday gift giving season approaches, consider a different type of gifting this year. Organizations that provide the raw materials of a sustainable existence, like goats, water, chickens, seeds and yes, guinea pigs, are much in need of our assistance to meet the needs of the neediest among us. Organizations like World Vision and Heifer International—just to name two—have put in place gift-giving programs to support a collective common good on the planet. Maybe the shopping we do this season could benefit someone thousands of miles away. We may never meet them, but on a very important level, we have connected with them for a life time.

Alright, let's really do something . . .

Adults – Seriously ask yourself how you model the art of giving. No one can tell you how much or to whom to give—that is a question we answer individually. When so much need exists in the world today, what we can say is that collectively we have not given enough.

Kids – Discover how you can make a difference in another kid's life. Are there any kids you know who are not as well off as you? How might you help them?

Together – Go through the shopping catalogs of organizations that help around the world or right here at home. Pick out something and buy a gift for someone who has real need.

For more info . . .

Life Saving:
http://goo.gl/UKFQ3

Wildlife Conservation:
http://goo.gl/4bx4i

Honey Bears,

What is extinct? It kind of sounds like stinky, but I think it is more important than stinky.

When we went on our trip the Big One talked about it a lot. He said we were staying in a place where the animals were becoming extincted or extinctified or something like that, but not stinky. This made him very concerned and even sad. He was hoping to see a certain bird through his big double big eye tubes that he said was near extinction. There, that's the word. Extinction.

I am not exactly sure what it means, I can tell the Big One knows it is serious.

Luff, Gizmo

145

What about us humans?

Our appreciation for those species that are on endangered lists has become heightened lately as more and more species are added to this roster. Many more are added than removed. To see an animal or plant in its native habitat is a thrilling experience. We must support conservation efforts that allow the planet to retain this level of integrity of preservation, for our children and their children. This is a common sense for common good move which will live for generations to come.

Alright, let's really do something . . .

Adults – Is there a zoo, aquarium, conservation group or animal rights organization you can support or volunteer for? Identify a species you love and help it to survive.

Kids – Learn about a specific extinct species and why it is extinct. Learn about a species that is on the endangered list and why it is endangered. Is there anything we can do to prevent this species from becoming a part of the extinct list?

Together – Take an eco trip if only in your imagination. Where would you go and what endangered animals do you want to see? Go to the library or sit down in front of a computer and look them up.

For more info . . .

Endangered Creatures:
http://goo.gl/VPM8B

Ecotourism:
http://goo.gl/cwX93

My Luffs,

Remember how I showed you a picture of my very own toy store?

I have not added very many lately. Mostly, I have been going around the place to find the ones I played with real hard and somehow lost. I have found my stray toys under the bed, between the cushions on the couch, under the table by a pile of the Lady's papers, and between the oatmeal box and the sugar jar in the pantry. (I'm still looking for Limpy if you spot him.)

The Big One says I don't NEED any more toys. Well, I know I don't NEED any more toys. I have got a whole bunch I haven't played with in some time and you are welcome to them. If no one asks for them soon, I am going to donate them. Ho, ho, ho!

Luff, Gizmo

What about us humans?

We all seem to accumulate stuff way past our level of real need. Some of it is sentimental, some of it historical, some just plain beautiful, and some, well, you fill in the blank. Most of us probably have too much. At celebration time we might think about donating rather than accumulating. Many organizations exist for us to recycle the stuff of our lives. Some will even come right to your home to pick it up. Check out the ones in your area. Ask a neighbor or a friend. Common sense for common good means putting our resources (even the used ones) to good use.

Alright, let's really do something . . .

Adults – Clean up and clean out and pass on. Remember a good rule of thumb is that if you bring something new into your home, send something out to someone in need.

Kids – Make a pile of things that you no longer use or want and find out where you can donate them. Have a day where you and all your buddies do the same.

Together – Try a shopping trip that does not involve "new." Go to a thrift store, an antique store, a garage sale, a yard sale. See what you can find that fills a need for you or someone else.

For more info . . .

Goodwill donations:
http://goo.gl/5vmnk

Savation Army:
http://goo.gl/WwS5N

Little Guys,

When it is very cold outside and you can hear the wind howling, my Lady likes to take a warm bath in her big sink before she goes to bed.

I know she likes this, but I like this time, too. I sit on the edge and watch the water rush into the tub and make bubbles. She smells so good after she comes out of the tub and after she dries off, she smears some special bottle stuff on her paws and her face.

I know she gets relaxed 'cuz after just a few minutes under the covers

This isn't the sort of bath I was referring to, but that maniac Chris seems to think it is in some way funny. Well he's English, what more can I say?

in bed, boy, she's sound asleep. She sleeps all curled up under the covers. Sometimes I sleep near to her on my back. We are both soon off to dreamland.

Luff, Gizmo

What about us humans?

How do you relax? Why do we need to relax? Our world can be a very hectic one. Having something in your repertoire to use when the day has been a long one, or the muscles are just very sore, is an important common sense move to keep handy. Cats have an innate ability to turn off the world and just nap—seemingly anywhere and anytime. We humans can also benefit from healing/rejuvenating experiences. Just make sure that the scents and products you are using are healthy for you and the planet. Choose natural, not synthetic or petroleum based options. Make your time for relaxation truly healthy. Remember, if you can't pronounce it and do not know what it is, why are you using it? Some of the most common personal care products contain harmful ingredients. Know what you are using.

Alright, let's really do something . . .

Adults – Take some time to learn about the art and science of scent. There are natural scents that can relax you or, conversely, energize you.

Kids – Take a nice warm bath and sing a lullaby to your favorite cat, dog or teddy.

Together – Take time to _____ (fill in the blank.) Find a mutually relaxing and rejuvenating activity like reading a book, walking around the block, baking some cookies . . . just connect and chill.

For more info . . .

Relaxation for Children:
http://goo.gl/vXx8A

Warm Kitty:
http://goo.gl/kmZJa

Punkins,

These piles of flat colored thingers come in with the Big One when he brings in the mail for the Lady. I have heard the Big One say on more than one occasion that this is a total waste.

What's a "total waste?" All I know is that this "total waste" doesn't spend much time in our home. It goes right back out into the cold and into the garage and in the box with all the rest of the "total waste." If I were a "total waste," I wouldn't want to come to our home. You're not welcome here.

Luff, Gizmo

KOUANG·TCHÉOU

INDOCHINE 1 5 CENT

RF

NGUYEN·HUU·DAU   LA JONQUE   G.DAUSSY

Now I know
he has
gone mad!
Boats? He
is trying
to ruin my
book!

What about us humans?

How much junk mail do you receive? For every household the answer varies. Many households have reduced the amount of junk mail they receive over time by taking their names off lists that send this type of mail. One can also request that billing statements be sent by email—this also reduces the amount of paper received in the mail. Many people read the daily news online as well. A reduction of paper use, and the resources needed for its manufacture, makes sense as these resources become more and more scarce.

Alright, let's really do something . . .

Adults – Help someone you know, who finds computers difficult to handle, to stop junk mail, or get their statements online. Often, all that is needed is a friendly explanation and a modicum of patience to see them through the process.

Kids – Help with the recycling and make sure all the paper (including your school papers that are not being saved) makes it into recycling bins at home or at school.

Together – Use paper sparingly. Use the back sides of paper for scratch paper, use the funny pages to wrap gifts, use newspaper to fill shipping boxes (not plastic peanuts), use cloth napkins, use a rag to wipe up (not paper towels), use a hand towel to dry off (not a paper towel) . . . Get it?

For more info . . .

Getting Rid of Junk Mail:
http://goo.gl/I4QOc

Paper Recycling:
http://goo.gl/nadrv

You Youngins,

My New Year's revolution is to calculate how many treats I can have in one day and still maintain my handsome physique.

The treat bags have the information I need to know, I just can't decipher it. I am going to ask the Big One to show me how the number box works and have him get the information off my favorite bag of treats. The Lady sometimes uses this number box to figure out what she calls a "price per serving." I know my treat bags have a lot of letters and numbers on them 'cuz I've seen 'em close up. Don't tell my humans.

When I get to the bottom of all this, I will fill you in on the details of my findings.

Luff, Gizmo

Nutrition Facts

Serv ng Size   Scoop (28g)
Servings Per Conta ner about 32

Amount Per Serving

Calories 0	**Ca ories from Fat** 25

	% Da ly Value*
Tota Fat 2 5g	**4**%
Saturated Fa g	**5**%
Trans F at 0g	
Cholesterol 65mg	**22**%
Sodium 70mg	**3**%
Potassium 50mg	**4**%
Tota Carbohydrate 3g	**1**%
Dietary F ber 0g	**0**%
Sugars g	
Protein 20g	**35**%

Vitam n A 0%   0%

Calc um   5%

*Percent Daily Values are based on a 2
be higher or lower depending on you
                    Calories.

Total F at
   Sat Fat
Cholestero
Sodium
Potassium
Total Carbohydrate
   Dietary Fiber
Protein

Calories per gram:
Fat 9   Carbohydrate 4   Pro

What about us humans?

The beginning of a new year often lends itself to some self examination. Perhaps this year, we could pay closer attention to what is actually in our food and what we are paying for it. As food prices continue to rise, it seems prudent to buy the healthiest, most nutritious, and least expensive kinds of food available. If, for example, by buying in larger quantities and/or changing to a healthier, less processed form of breakfast cereal (idea–bulk raw oats instead of processed, boxed cereals), we can improve our lives–then why not? Take a look at what you are buying. Read the labels and crunch the numbers. Perhaps a change or two makes good common sense.

Alright, let's really do something . . .

Adults – Pick one meal, say breakfast, and one food, say cereal, and make the change to a healthier and more nutritious choice. Now try to buy that choice in bulk. Keep track of costs for a few months and see if your choice had positive results. Now choose another meal, and another food. Repeat. Continue repeating until the healthy, nutritious, and low cost food options are what fill your shopping cart.

Kids – Don't complain when the adults won't buy you junk food. There will come a day when you will thank your lucky stars they cared enough to put up with your complaining and didn't cave in.

Together – Try baking bread from scratch. Use healthy ingredients. Eat it while it is still warm, with jam.

For more info . . .

Cheap Healthy Foods:
http://goo.gl/x25e8

Healthy Cats:
http://goo.gl/27R6Q

My Best Buddies,

My humans have been making some balls for my outside friends to eat. Food is hard to find at this time of the year.

The balls they made have brown sticky gooey stuff from this jar smeared all over them and they are covered with some seeds. They use the same seeds that they feed the birds outside. It is a very messy project. The Lady lets me watch, but she says I would end up a sticky mess if I helped her.

Remember Snowman, my squirrel friend? I am going to signal him when I know my humans are going to put these balls outside. I try to keep him informed about things that might interest him. You know we all need to work together.

Luff, Gizmo

165

What about us humans?

Winter can be especially hard on our outdoor animal neighbors. Many species do not migrate, but stay with us year round. Providing high energy treats like suet or handmade peanut butter seed balls can enhance the lives of those living in the cold elements. We can connect with the animals that live around us by remembering them and providing for them. A beautiful bird silhouetted against the white of a new snow fall is a wonder to behold in the dark of winter.

Alright, let's really do something . . .

Adults – Connect, connect, and connect with nature. The benefits of a life infused with the gifts of Mother Nature have been well documented. Whether you feed the pigeons, or walk a dog, or plant a flower, or lie on your back and watch the cloud pictures, nature is a wonder to behold. Get out and enjoy it.

Kids – Share your peanut butter with our outdoor feathered friends. They will thank you in their own special ways.

Together – Make a peanut butter seed ball.

For more info . . .

Bird Seed Balls:
http://goo.gl/HMyvs

Garden for Wildlife:
http://goo.gl/v2Bzm

Here's your bird! Wow, it will be good to get that cat off my back!

Gizmosims

I have made this list so that you can understand some of my unusual words.

banky—my pink blanket
bankys—lots of them
bemember—remember
big black box—microwave
big blasty hot air thingy—furnace
big hot white box—dryer
big round circles—plates
big sink—the Lady's bath tub
big white box—washing machine
boxy black and white squares—QR codes
brown squares—slices of bread
brown sticky gooey stuff—peanut butter
coinkidinky—coincidence
Cool Lady—Barbara
cool round bowl—bathroom sink
crinkly paper—wax paper
dark brown speckles—ground coffee
degees—a measure of air temperature
disgustapating—really awful
double big black eye tubes—binoculars
extincted/extictified—variations of extinction, as in gone forever
fancy wrapping—packaging
felinexology—cat version of reflexology
flat colored thingers—newspaper ads, junk mail
flat paper stiff thingy—furnace filter
flip side—some time soon
foldy thing—drying rack
fuggetabowtit—forget about it, as in late for cake
giant screen—patio window
goop—toothpaste
Granny—the Lady's mama
human purring—snoring

ingedients—what is in the stuff
intellectrical—combination of intelligent and electric as in work
invincable—invisible
knickers—underwear
Limpy—one of, if not my favorite, toy . . . he is missing some parts
long tail—electric cord and plug
luff—love
noisemakers—jungle animals
noisy wheeled machine—vacuum cleaner
nubbins—food crumbs
number box—calculator
number dial thingy—thermostat
personal cable network channel—my view of the back yard
play box for the Big One—garden
pointy silver sticks—forks
pooling—car pooling
private box—litter box
pooter—computer
reflection windows—mirrors
revolution—kind of like a resolution only it has more impact
silver stick—tire pressure gauge
snipples—dry food pieces
special bottle stuff—the Lady's lotion
stuff from play box—vegetables
TeeVahDee—television
the Lady—Karen
the Big One—Charles
total waste—junk mail
viewing screen—patio window
vitimazation—healthy eating
wambo—real fast
wipper snapper—young in experience

Gratitude

No cat makes a book like this on his own. I had the help of many paws along the way.

As far as book designers go, my pal Chris, the magnifico, is one of the best. His particular skill set enabled him to translate my letters purrrrfectly. Most of the mess on the pages, though, is his fault entirely. I desperately tried to rein him in, but to no avail.

Miss Judith helped my Lady with her pooter letters and made sure she was tapping the keys in the right order. She's smart with the pooters, you know, and ohhhh, so nice.

Woocy and Skip did some helping with the letters, too. Maybe I can meet them some day, although I hear Woocy is not too fond of fur. I'll have me a comb out before I see her.

My first mama number one and mama number two, MJ and Sofia, helped me make it to the two best humans I ever met, the Lady and the Big One. For that, I am soooooooooo happy. Without them, well, you wouldn't be reading this book.

So, great big thanks to all the humans who helped me put this book together. I couldn't have done it without you. Well, maybe I could have, but it wouldn't have been half as much fun.

Luff, Gizmo

OK that's all from me. I'll let the Lady write the final words.

169

Outroduction

I cannot recall a time in my life when I was not in a daily connection with animals. They have been my teachers and my companions through some of the most harrowing experiences in my life and have been constant sources of unconditional love, kindness, and acceptance. Every living being is connected, and things such as the care and tenderness expressed through a relationship with an animal are the same energies that unite us all and with the planet itself. These are the ties that bind and they are much greater than what divides us.

In expressing Gizmo's story, I embark upon another effort to emphasize how profoundly connected we are. There are many kinds of storytellers in this world. The philosophers, the cartoonists, the scientists, the painters, the astronomers—they all have a story to tell and it is our story. They use different words, different media, and different understandings to tell our story. What they have in common, what we all have in common, is the journey. The journey we are all on, and desperately trying to help each other through. The storytellers understand our connections. They understand them, and try to reflect them back to us—and we ponder, oh how we ponder.

We live in a world filled with tremendous challenges. We live with daily reminders of how much needs to be addressed on our planet. Every once in a while we need to look at ourselves and figure out, once again, what needs to be changed. The very serious intent of this book is to collectively move us to a place where we accept our role as the catalyst necessary to make this world one we want to live in. Maybe, just maybe, the eyes and attitude of a cat named Gizmo will help us do just that.

Spending a lifetime with an animal as a pet teaches us to accept change. For no matter how much we fight it, it is inevitable. My husband and I vowed we would never have another cat when Azure Blue died, for her passing broke our hearts. A couple of years later, when Gizmo peaked out of a red wool bag and looked into our eyes for the first time, we at once became hooked again and were connected for life with that tiny ball of fur.

Those universal energies of love and unconditional acceptance are what will get us out of this mess we find ourselves in—that and a little humor. If a purring, very furry, long gray-haired, green-eyed cat named Gizmo can help save the planet, well then, who better?

Karen Olson Johnson

Conclusion . . . just a note.

The world is blessed by those whose words are tied with actions. Our future is the one we are willing to create. For Gizmo, and all the kitties that will follow, let's hope it is a world of luff.

Appendix 1

Observations by number, including page numbers, TOPICS, and related observation numbers.

Obs 1 (page 8): Switching to larger CONTAINERS (9, 13,32)

Obs 2 (page 12): Reducing phantom ENERGY/ELECTRICITY (11)

Obs 3 (page 16): Saving precious WATER (8)

Obs 4 (page 20): Trying CAR POOLING (20)

Obs 5 (page 24): Air DRYING LAUNDRY (2, 11)

Obs 6 (page 28): Turning off LIGHTS (11)

Obs 7 (page 32): Adjusting the THERMOSTATS (24)

Obs 8 (page 36): Using WASTE WATER (3)

Obs 9 (page 40): Bringing REUSABLE BAGS (13)

Obs 10 (page 44): COMPOSTING food waste (33)

Obs 11 (page 48): Installing EFFICIENT LIGHTING (6)

Obs 12 (page 52): Valuing MOTHER NATURE (22, 28, 40)

Obs 13 (page 56): Making an ECO-FRIENDLY LUNCH (9, 14, 17, 32, 39)

Obs 14 (page 60): Banning DISPOSABLES from meals (13, 32)

Obs 15 (page 64): Starting PAPER RECYCLING (38)

Obs 16 (page 68): Doing proper ELECTRONIC RECYCLING (23)

Obs 17 (page 72): Eating ORGANIC FOODS (18, 32)

Obs 18 (page 76): Growing FOOD in your GARDENS (12,17)

Obs 19 (page 80): CONNECTING with each other (29, 34, 35, 36, 37, 40)

Obs 20 (page 84): Maintaining EFFICIENT VEHICLES (4)

Obs 21 (page 88): CLEANING sinks with safe PRODUCTS (26)

Obs 22 (page 92): Supporting LIVING THINGS (12)

Obs 23 (page 96): Accumulating STUFF (34, 36)

Obs 24 (page 100): Increasing HEATING EFFICIENCY (7)

Obs 25 (page 104): Keeping indoor AIR healthy (21, 26)

Obs 26 (page 108): Household non-toxic CLEANING (21, 25)

Obs 27 (page 112): TRAVELLING with the planet in mind (30)
Obs 28 (page 116): Learning about ECOSYSTEMS (12, 22, 30, 35, 40)
Obs 29 (page 120): CONNECTING through the practice of MEDITATION (19, 37)
Obs 30 (page 124): Planting TREES (12, 22)
Obs 31 (page 128): Installing WEATHER STRIPPING (7, 24)
Obs 32 (page 132): EATING slow or fast food (17, 18, 39)
Obs 33 (page 136): COMPOSTING leaves (10)
Obs 34 (page 140): GIVING to others (23, 40)
Obs 35 (page 144): PROTECTING the animals (12, 28, 40)
Obs 36 (page 148): DONATING all the stuff (23, 34)
Obs 37 (page 152): Healthy RELAXING (19, 29)
Obs 38 (page 156): Wasting PAPER (15, 30)
Obs 39 (page 160): EATING more cheaply and more healthily (13, 18)
Obs 40 (page 164): Helping other ANIMALS (12, 22, 28, 35)

Appendix 2

Observations by TOPIC, related topic numbers, observation number, and page number.

Keeping indoor AIR healthy (21, 26): Obs 25 (page 104)
Helping other ANIMALS (12, 22, 28, 35): Obs 40 (page 164)
Trying CAR POOLING (20): Obs 4 (page 20)
Household non-toxic CLEANING (21, 25): Obs 26 (page 108)
CLEANING sinks with safe PRODUCTS (26): Obs 21 (page 88)
COMPOSTING food waste (33): Obs 10 (page 44)
COMPOSTING leaves (10): Obs 33 (page 136)
CONNECTING through the practice of MEDITATION (19, 37): Obs 29 (page 120)
CONNECTING with each other (29, 34, 35, 36, 37, 40): Obs 19 (page 80)
Switching to larger CONTAINERS (9, 13,32): Obs 1 (page 8)

Banning DISPOSABLES from meals (13, 32): Obs 14 (page 60)

DONATING all the stuff (23, 34): Obs 36 (page 148)

Air DRYING LAUNDRY (2, 11): Obs 5 (page 24)

EATING more cheaply and more healthily (13, 18): Obs 39 (page 160)

EATING slow or fast food (17, 18, 39): Obs 32 (page 132)

Making an ECO-FRIENDLY LUNCH (9, 14, 17, 32, 39): Obs 13 (page 56)

Learning about ECOSYSTEMS (12, 22, 30, 35, 40): Obs 28 (page 116)

Installing EFFICIENT LIGHTING (6): Obs 11 (page 48)

Maintaining EFFICIENT VEHICLES (4): Obs 20 (page 84)

Doing proper ELECTRONIC RECYCLING (23): Obs 16 (page 68)

Reducing phantom ENERGY/ELECTRICITY (11): Obs 2 (page 12)

Growing FOOD in your GARDENS (12,17): Obs 18 (page 76)

GIVING to others (23, 40): Obs 34 (page 140)

Increasing HEATING EFFICIENCY (7): Obs 24 (page 100)

Turning off LIGHTS (11): Obs 6 (page 28)

Supporting LIVING THINGS (12): Obs 22 (page 92)

Valuing MOTHER NATURE (22, 28, 40): Obs 12 (page 52)

Eating ORGANIC FOODS (18, 32): Obs 17 (page 72)

Wasting PAPER (15, 30): Obs 38 (page 156)

Starting PAPER RECYCLING (38): Obs 15 (page 64)

PROTECTING the animals (12, 28, 40): Obs 35 (page 144)

Healthy RELAXING (19, 29): Obs 37 (page 152)

Bringing REUSABLE BAGS (13): Obs 9 (page 40)

Accumulating STUFF (34, 36): Obs 23 (page 96)

Adjusting the THERMOSTATS (24): Obs 7 (page 32)

TRAVELLING with the planet in mind (30): Obs 27 (page 112)

Planting TREES (12, 22): Obs 30 (page 124)

Using WASTE WATER (3): Obs 8 (page 36)

Saving precious WATER (8): Obs 3 (page 16)

Installing WEATHER STRIPPING (7, 24): Obs 31 (page 128)

Bio

Karen Olson Johnson chooses to live sustainably. With her scientific, academic, and mentoring expertise, she is a powerful advocate for the earth and its creatures. Karen spreads her important message through awareness, education, and action. As an author (*Common Sense for Common Good*) and consultant, Karen uses multiple media to reach her audience. Karen has the heart of a storyteller and speaks with a prophetic voice. She truly believes if we care enough to change ourselves, we will change the world. She lives with Gizmo and the Big One (her husband Charles) and a few other animal buddies in Minnesota.

Feedback

We would appreciate hearing from you if you have comments to make or other useful links to suggest.

www.commonsenseforcommongood.net

ISBN: 978-1-61766-202-7

Conceived by Karen Olson Johnson and Chris Fayers

Editor: Judith Palmateer

Photo credits: Karen Olson Johnson, Charles Johnson, Shirley Olson, 123RF, PhotoXpress, Douglas Fayers and Chris Fayers